THIS WALKER BOOK BELONGS TO:

For thousands of years,
fishermen have watched every autumn
as adult eels migrated down rivers into the sea,
and again every spring as the young eels returned.
But nobody knew what happened in between.
Where did the adults go to?
And where were the young eels born?
Today we think we know the secret of the eel,
but even now no one has ever seen a wild
eel lay eggs or an eel egg hatch.

For Martin Llewellyn
K. W.

For my Dad
M. B.

First published 1993
by Walker Books Ltd
87 Vauxhall Walk
London SE11 5HJ

10 9 8 7 6 5 4 3 2

Text © 1993 Karen Wallace
Illustrations © 1993 Mike Bostock

Printed in Hong Kong

British Library Cataloguing
in Publication Data:
a catalogue record for
this book is available
from the British Library

ISBN 0-7445-6270-8

THINK of an EEL

Karen Wallace

illustrated by
Mike Bostock

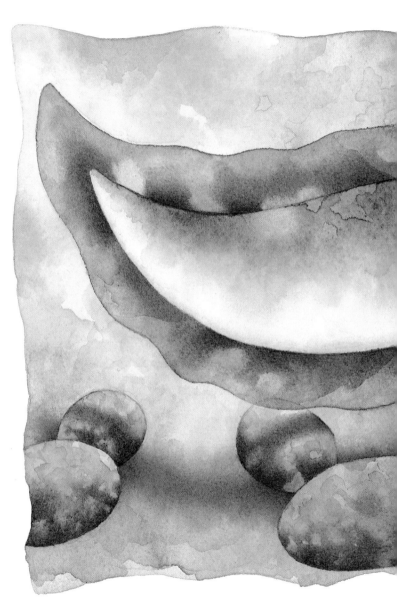

WALKER BOOKS
AND SUBSIDIARIES
LONDON • BOSTON • SYDNEY

Think of an eel.

He swims like a fish.

He slides like a snake.

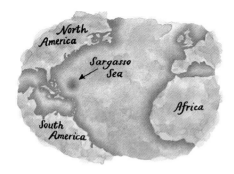

There's a warm, weedy sea
to the south of Bermuda.
It's called the Sargasso.
No wind ever blows there,
no sailing ships sail there.
For thousands of years there
a secret lay hidden:
this salt, soupy sea
is where eels are born.
Deep down where it's blackest,
eel egg becomes eel.
He looks like a willow leaf,
clear as a crystal.

Baby eels are born in early spring.
A real one is only

about this big.

8

His fierce jutting mouth
has teeth like a sawblade.

He eats like a horse and
swims up through the water.

Young eels from the Sargasso travel either to Europe or to America – whichever

their parents did before them.

Imagine this eel-leaf
and millions just like him
swimming on waves
across the wide sea.
Some are unlucky.
The seagulls are waiting.
Beaks snap like scissors
through wriggling water.

Eel swims for three years
till he reaches the shore

but the river's too cold, there's
still snow on the mountains.

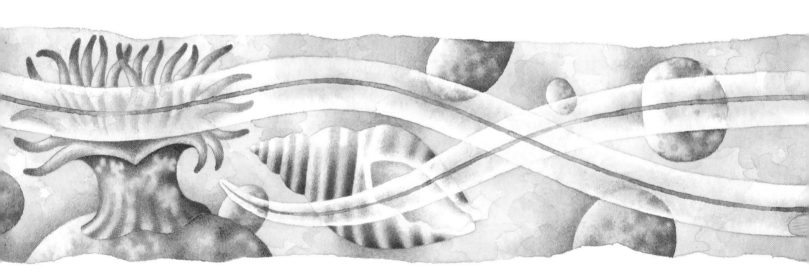

Eels arrive in Europe around Christmas time. They wait offshore

So he waits in the water,
turns into an elver.

Now he looks like a shoelace
made out of glass.

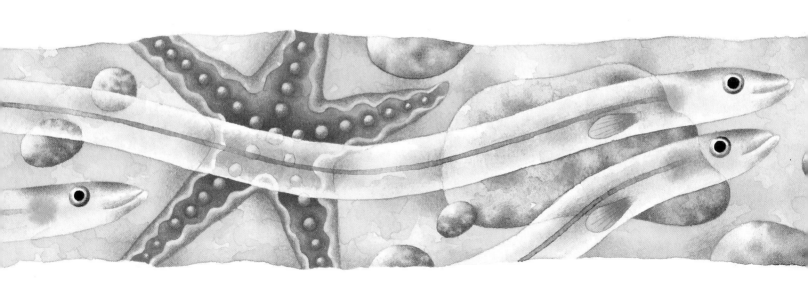

until spring, and as they wait they turn into elvers.

When spring
warms the shoreline,
the smell of fresh water
excites the glass elver.
Into the river
he swims like a mad thing.
He wriggles up rapids,
climbs rocks
around waterfalls.
River banks guide him.
Nothing will stop him.

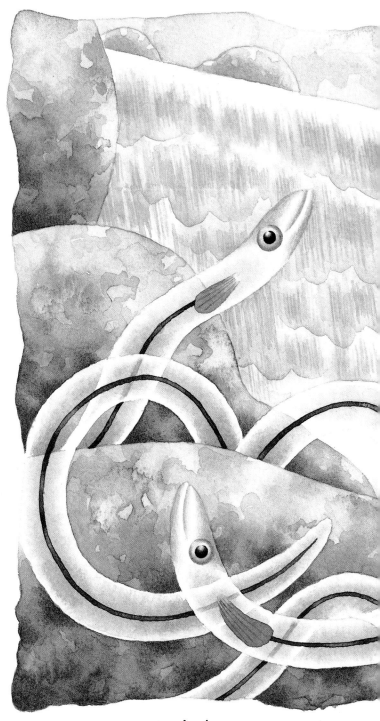

Eels navigate by instinct.

They always seem to know where they are going.

Around a drowned oak stump,
through twisting green weeds,
a mudhole is hidden.

Mudholes, burrows and cracks in the river bed are all homes for eels.

Eel knows without thinking
it's what he's been seeking.
He slips through the ooze.
This hole is his home.

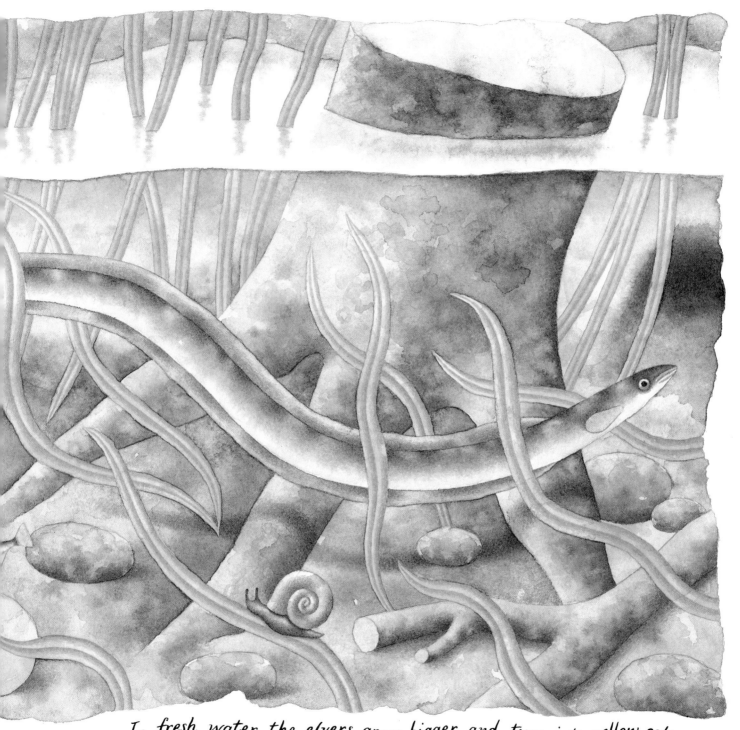

In fresh water, the elvers grow bigger and turn into yellow eels.

Think of an eel.
After years in the river
he's slit-eyed and slimy
and thick like a snake.
He gulps stickleback eggs,
eats shrimps and small fishes.

shrimp

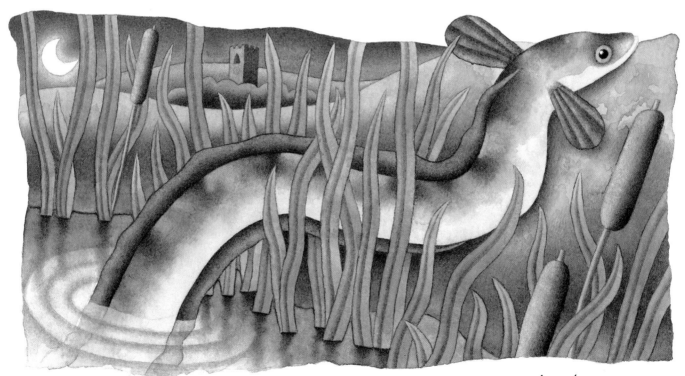

Eels feed mostly at night.

If the river is empty

he swims from the mudhole,

slips through the grass

to steal snails from the pond.

pond snail

An eel can live out of water for two days or longer, if the ground is wet, breathing through its slimy skin.

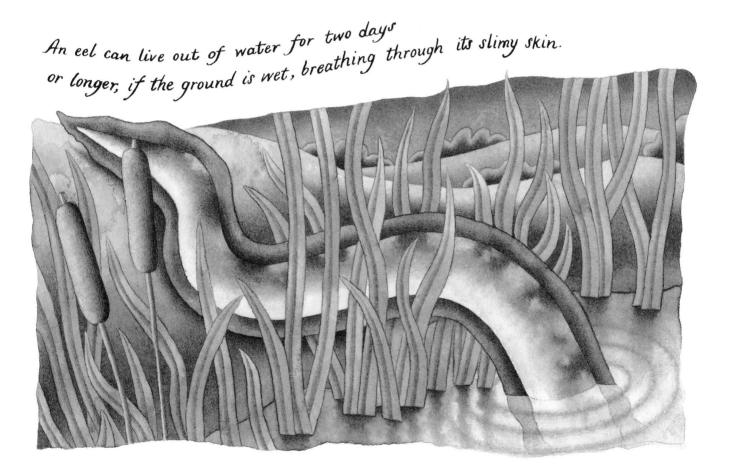

One day eel stops eating.

His stomach is shrinking.

His long winding body

turns silver and black.

Eyes like blackcurrants

bulge into headlamps.

Now for the last time

eel slides from the mudhole.

His years in the river

are over for ever.

Silver eels usually leave the river in September or October.

Silver eel waits

for a night that is moonless,

when the rain from the mountains

has flooded the stream.

22

While they're waiting for a dark night, they sometimes get tangled up in a ball.

Then he slips
down the river, down to
the seashore. The time has arrived
for his long journey home.

For eighty days

silver eel swims through the ocean,

squirms like a secret

from seabird and sailor.

There are millions just like him,
deep down in the water,
swimming silently back
to the Sargasso Sea.

big eyes for seeing in the dark

25

There's eel-tomb and eel-cradle
in the weedy Sargasso.
After eighty days' swimming,
not eating, not sleeping,
eel's long, winding body
is worn out and wasted.
He spills the new life
carried deep in his belly,
then sinks through the sea
like a used silver wrapper.

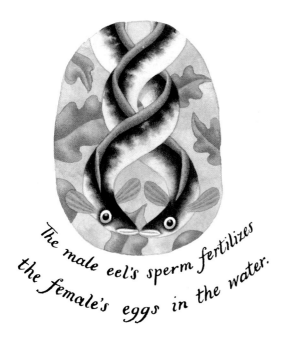

The male eel's sperm fertilizes the female's eggs in the water.

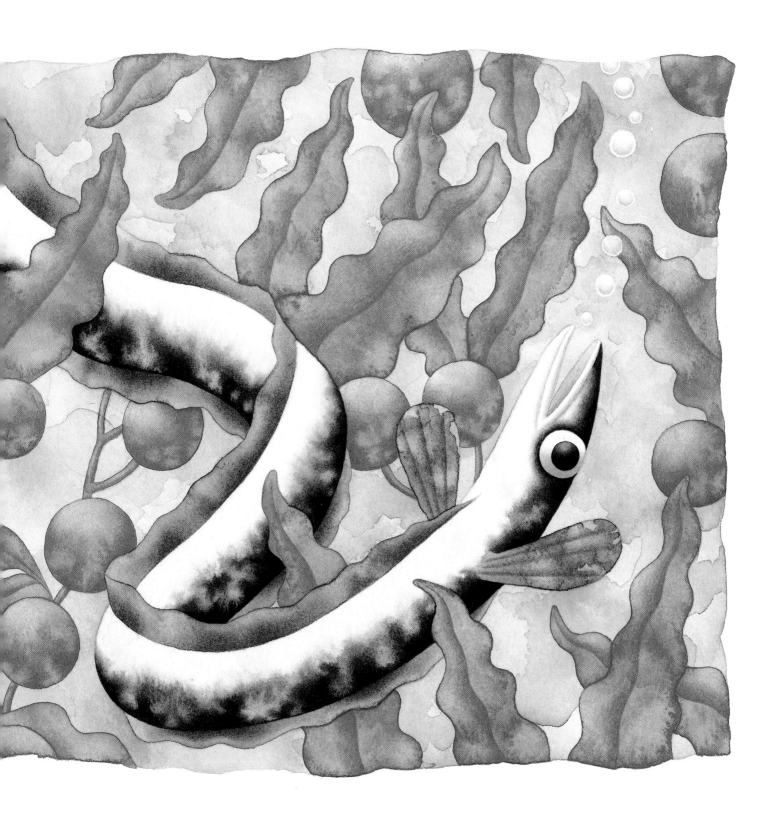

Deep down where it's blackest,

eel egg becomes eel.

He looks like a willow leaf,

clear as a crystal.

His fierce jutting mouth

has teeth like a sawblade.

He eats like a horse and

swims up through the water.

Imagine this eel-leaf

and millions just like him

swimming on waves

across the wide sea…

Index

Look up the pages to find
out about all these eel things. Don't
forget to look at both kinds of words:
this kind *and this kind*.

A note from the author

Karen Wallace has always
been fascinated by eels.
"Their story is magical and
truly mysterious," she says.
"Even today, the spawning
grounds of some eel
species are still
unknown..."

A note from
the illustrator

Mike Bostock remembers
from his youth strange
myths about the origin of eels.
"They sprang from horse's tails
dipped in the river or from the mud of
the riverbed," he says. "Reading Karen's
text, I was captivated by the fact that
the eel had a life story as
extraordinary as those myths,
and I tried to put that feeling
into my pictures."

NOTES FOR TEACHERS

The READ AND WONDER series is an innovative and versatile resource for reading, thinking and discovery. Each book invites children to become excited about a topic, see how varied information books can be, and want to find out more.

☞ **Reading aloud** The story form makes these books ideal for reading aloud – in their own right or as part of a cross-curricular topic, to a child or to a whole class. After you've introduced children to the books in this way, they can revisit and enjoy them again and again.

☞ **Shared reading** Big Book editions are available for several titles, so children can read along, discuss the topic, and comment on the different ways information is presented – to wonder together.

☞ **Group and guided reading** Children need to experience a range of reading materials. Information books like these help develop the skills of reading to learn, as part of learning to read. With the support of a reading group, children can become confident, flexible readers.

☞ **Paired reading** It's fun to take turns to read the information in the main text or captions. With a partner, children can explore the pages to satisfy their curiosity and build their understanding.

☞ **Individual reading** These books can be read for interest and pleasure by children at home and in school.

☞ **Research** Once children have been introduced to these books through reading aloud, they can use them for independent or group research, as part of a curricular topic.

☞ **Children's own writing** You can offer these books as strong models for children's own information writing. They can record their observations and findings about a topic, make field notes and sketches, and add extra snippets of information for the reader.

Above all, Read and Wonders are to be enjoyed, and encourage children to develop a lasting curiosity about the world they live in.

Sue Ellis, Centre for Language in Primary Education